KISS [illegible] NOT ME!

JUNKO

CONTENTS

STORY

KAE PRIORITIZES THE **"MIRAGE SAGA"** EVENT AND BREAKS HER PROMISE TO MEET **MUTSUMI**. **KAE** IS TORN WHEN **MUTSUMI** ASKS HER IF SHE LIKES HIM OR SHION MORE. BUT WHEN **KAE** FINDS OUT THAT **YASHIRO** IS GETTING CLOSER TO **MUTSUMI**, SHE REALIZES THAT IT'S **MUTSUMI** SHE LIKES MORE THAN ANYONE ELSE. THE TWO REVEAL HOW THEY FEEL ABOUT EACH OTHER AND MAKE UP. ON TOP OF THAT, **MUTSUMI** RIPS UP HIS TRAIN TICKET, SAYING THAT **HE DOESN'T WANT TO BE APART FROM HER ANYMORE!**

I ♥ BL

CHARACTER
THE MAIN CHARACTER—A FUJOSHI WITH WILD FANTASIES
SHE'S CRAZY ABOUT THE ANIME "MIRAGE SAGA." ❤ CURRENTLY IN A RELATIONSHIP WITH MUTSUMI-SENPAI.
SERINUMA KAE 芹沼花依
THE SPORTY CLASSMATE
ON THE SOCCER TEAM. THE POPULAR KID IN CLASS. HE'S SECRETLY TAKEN KAE TO A SPOT WITH A BEAUTIFUL NIGHT VIEW.
IGARASHI YUSUKE 五十嵐祐輔
THE FRIVOLOUS CLASSMATE
FORMERLY ON THE SOCCER TEAM. HE HAS A SMART MOUTH, BUT HE TELLS IT LIKE IT IS. HE STOLE A KISS FROM KAE WHILE HALF-ASLEEP.
NANASHIMA NOZOMU 七島希
THE SUB-CULTURE SENPAI
IN THE SAME HISTORY CLUB AS KAE. HE'S TREATED KAE THE SAME WAY AS HE DID IN THE BEGINNING. KAE'S FIRST BOYFRIEND.
MUTSUMI ASUMA 六見遊馬
THE HOT-N-COLD KOHAI
A MEMBER OF THE HEALTH COMMITTEE LIKE KAE. HIS GRANDFATHER IS NORWEGIAN. HE'S FALLEN INTO KAE'S CHEST TWICE.
SHINOMIYA HAYATO 四ノ宮隼人
NISHINA SHIMA 二科志麻
THE HANDSOME FEMALE KOHAI
AND KAE'S FELLOW FUJOSHI FRIEND. A SUPER RICH YOUNG LADY. SHE WAS KAE'S FIRST KISS.
MUTSUMI'S CLASSMATE, AND LEADER OF THE SHOGI CLUB. LIKE KAE, HE'S A FAN OF "MIRAGE SAGA."
YASHIRO ARATA 八城新

KiSS HiM, NOT ME!

#52 THEIR FIRST TIME?!

KiSS HiM,
NOT ME!

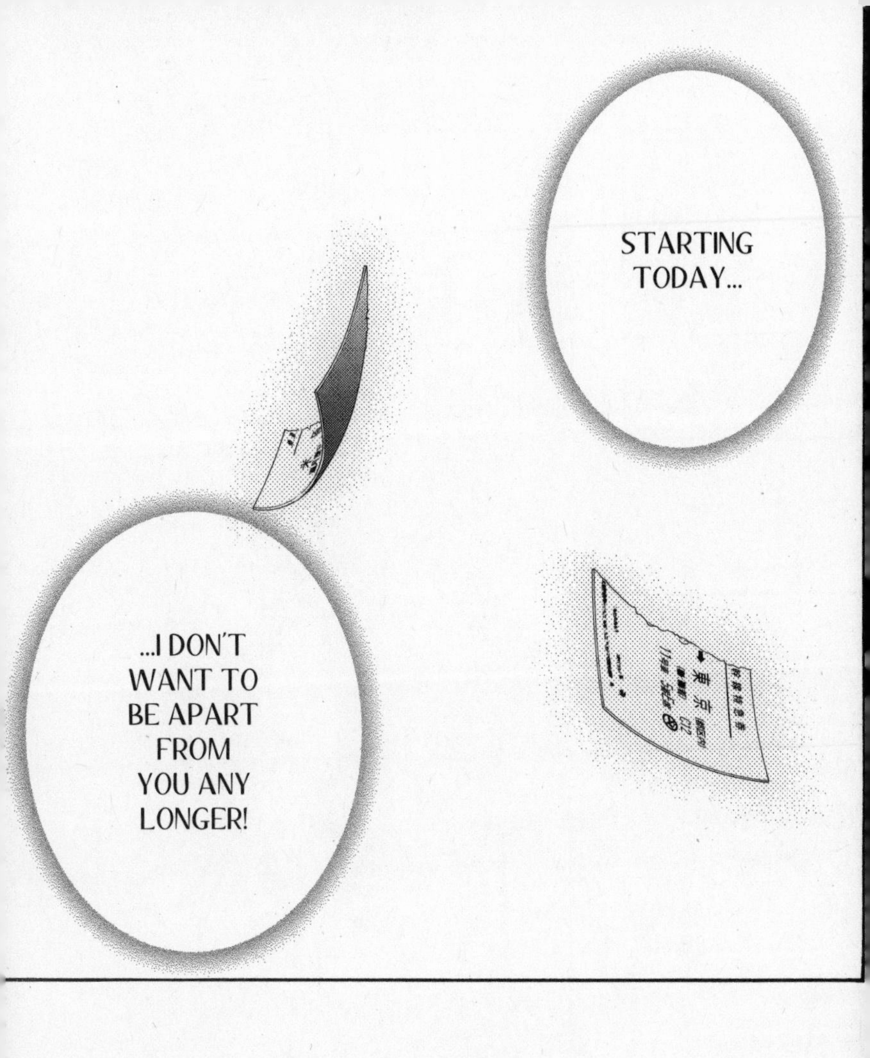

STARTING TODAY...
...I DON'T WANT TO BE APART FROM YOU ANY LONGER!

KiSS HiM, NOT ME!

HOTEL
RATE INN
FSSSHHH
FSSSHHH
I...

I GOT THIS FAR PURELY ON MOMENTUM, AND...
...N-NOW I'M HERE...
HOLD ON A SEC!!
FSSSHHH

AND THE ONLY ARMS I WANT TO BE IN...
...ARE YOURS, SENPAI!!
DID I BLURT OUT...
...SOME-THING CRAZY?!
EEEEEEEKK!!

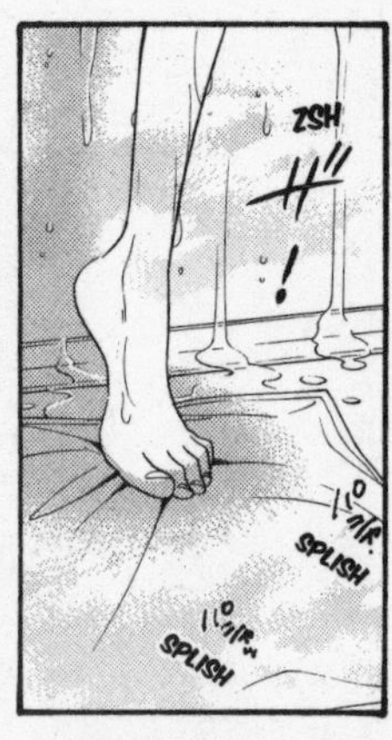
ZSH
SPLISH
SPLISH

C... COME TO THINK OF IT, I WASHED MY HAIR.
Gotta dry off quick...
Let's see...
I WONDER IF IT'S OKAY FOR ME TO WEAR THIS ROBE.

VWOOSH
BADUMP
BADUMP
FWOO
BADUMP
BA-
DUMP

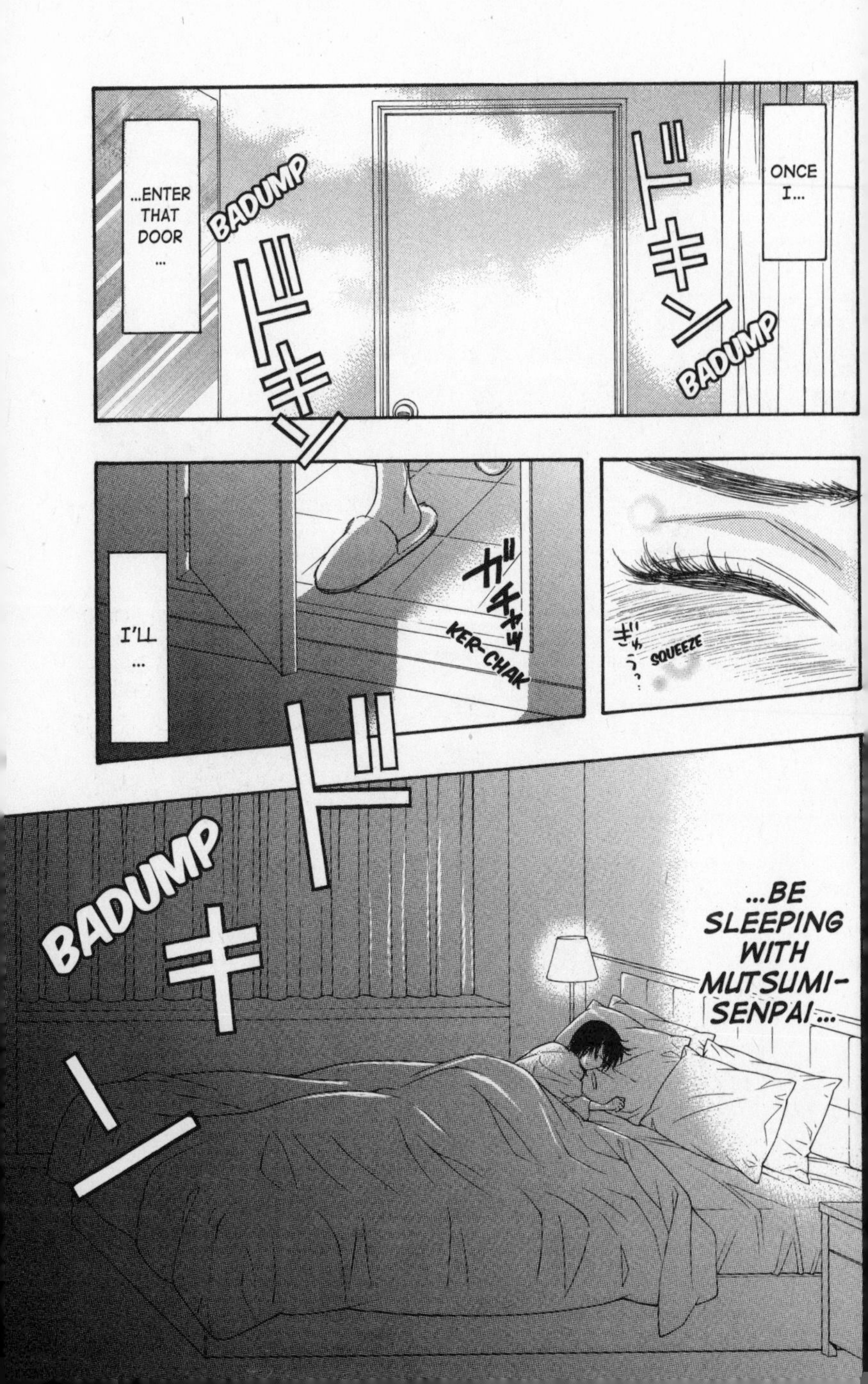
ONCE I...
ドキン
BADUMP
...ENTER THAT DOOR ...
BADUMP
ドキン
ぎゅう…
SQUEEZE
ガチャ
KER-CHAK
I'LL ...
...BE SLEEPING WITH MUTSUMI-SENPAI...
ドキン
BADUMP

HUH ...?
きょとん
FREEZE

ギッ...
CREAK...
Y...YOU'RE SLEEPING ...?
S... SEN-PAI?

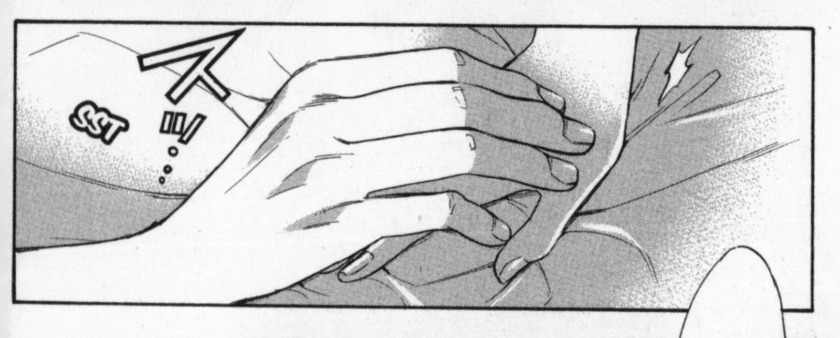
SST

I'M AWAKE.

BADUMP
UH...
FWUMP
BADUMP
BADUMP
BADUMP
I HAVEN'T BEEN THIS CLOSE TO YOU ...
...IN A REALLY LONG TIME, SERINUMA-SAN...

FOR COMING ALL THE WAY OUT HERE TO SEE ME.
THANKS.
A... ALL I COULD THINK ABOUT ...
...WAS HOW MUCH I MISSED YOU, SENPAI ...
...ABOUT HOW I HAD TO SEE YOU ...
I MISSED YOU, TOO...
CREAK
...!
TWITCH

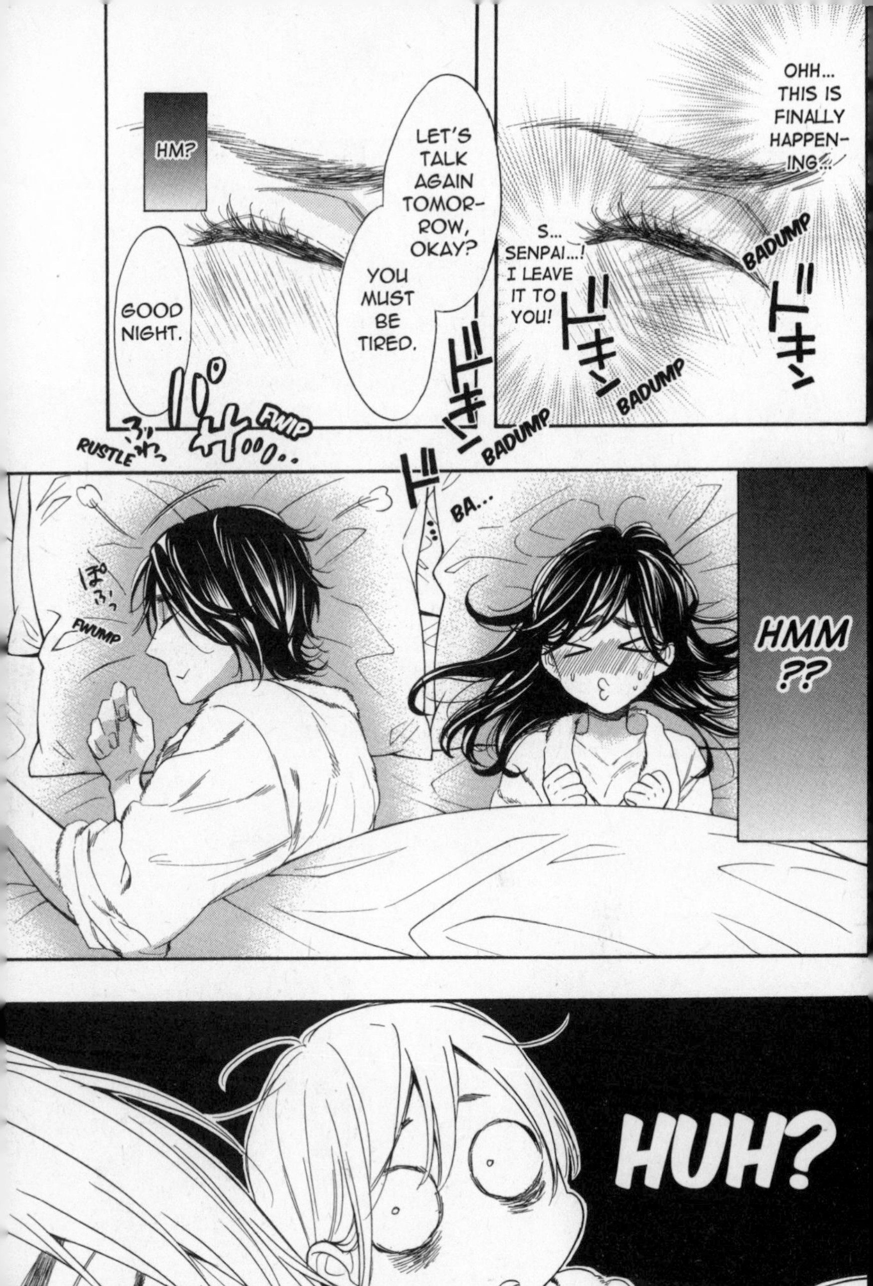

OHH... THIS IS FINALLY HAPPEN-ING...
BADUMP
ドキン
S... SENPAI...! I LEAVE IT TO YOU!
ドキン
BADUMP
LET'S TALK AGAIN TOMOR-ROW, OKAY?
YOU MUST BE TIRED.
HM?
GOOD NIGHT.
FWIP
RUSTLE
BADUMP
HMM ??
BA...
FWUMP

HUH?

HUH ...?
HUHHHHH ?!
HOTEL RATE INN

Tuesday rolls around.

Morning!
Good morning.
OH.

KAE-CHAAAN!! MOOOR-NING!!
YOU DIDN'T COME TO SCHOOL YESTER-DAY! SO HOW DID SUNDAY GO?
YOU WENT TO SHIGA, RIGHT? DID YOU TWO MAKE UP?!
OHH! OF COURSE YOU DID! THAT'S WHY YOU DIDN'T COME TO SCHOOL YESTER-DAY! HOW SILLY OF ME!! HA HA HA HA HA!
BLAB BLAB BLAB BLAB BLAB

OH.
YEAH, WE MADE UP. ☆
GLOOOM

HUH...?
REEL
DUN DUN DUN
YOU SURE DON'T LOOK LIKE YOU DID...
...

AH-CHAN! C'MON, LET'S GO!!
HUH?
HEY! KAE-CHAN?!
DASH

WH... WHAT IS IT? WHAT'S THE MATTER?!
DID SOMETHING HAPPEN?
PANT PANT
N... NOTHING HAPPENED...
HUH?

GYAHHHH
I WENT TO SHIGA, AND THEN WE POURED OUR HEARTS OUT TO EACH OTHER AND GOT CARRIED AWAY, AND THEN WE GOT A HOTEL ROOM, I TOOK A SHOWER, WE GOT INTO BED, AND HE WHISPERED SWEET NOTHINGS TO ME!!
AND THEN NOTH-ING!! NOTH-ING HAP-PENED!!!

WE JUST SLEPT NEXT TO EACH OTHER UNTIL MORN-ING!!
CHIRP
CHIRP
HUHHH ...?!
WHAAA ...?
???

AH-CHAN... IS...IS THIS... NOR-MAL ?
IS... IS IT NORMAL FOR TWO PEOPLE WHO HAVE FEELINGS FOR EACH OTHER TO SHARE A HOTEL ROOM TOGETH-ER...
...AND HAVE NOTH-ING HAP-PEN?
TEAR
TEAR

WELL... EVERYONE'S DIFFERENT, SO I CAN'T REALLY MAKE GENERALI-ZATIONS, BUT...
YEAH, IT MIGHT NOT BE NORMAL ...
RIGHT ?!
ACK

IF THIS WERE A BL MANGA, THEY WOULD ABSOLUTELY HAVE DONE IT, RIGHT?!
I'm not gonna let you sleep tonight...
Ohh...
WHY DIDN'T IT HAPPEN FOR US?! WHAT'S GOING ON?!
WAHHH!
Oh dear...
HEY, DON'T THINK ABOUT BL MANGA... I MEAN... WELL... UH...
WHY ...?
MY HEART WAS RACING... AND I WAS SO READY WHEN I FOLLOWED HIM...
DID SENPAI NOT FEEL THE SAME WAY...?
WAS I...NOT GOOD ENOUGH FOR HIM?
WAS I... NOT ABLE TO GET HIM IN THE MOOD?
A...AM I NOT... ATTRACTIVE?
DRIP
DRIP
KAE-CHAN ...
DING
DONG
DANG
DONG

ザワ
CHATTER
ザワ
CHATTER

...?

3-B
Yusuke Igarashi
I need to talk to you.
あ
か
さ
な
は
次候補
や
ら
CHATTER
ザワ
HMM
...
CHATTER
ザワ
CHATTER
ザワ

WHAT'S THE MATTER MUTSUMI?
HUH?

DID YOU MAKE UP WITH KAE SERINUMA?
ニコ… GRIN

UH, YEAH ... WE MADE UP.
HM. I SEE. Good to hear.
MU-TSUMI-SAAAN.

DO YOU HAVE A MINUTE ...?

IGA-RASHI-KUN!!
ガタッ CLATTER

YOU CAME AT JUST THE RIGHT TIME!
I HAVE SOMETHING TO TALK TO YOU ABOUT...
C'MON!!
WHA?
HUH?
DASH!
HUH?
HEY, UH, MUTSUMI-SAN?!
SERI-NUMA-SAN FOLLOWED YOU ALL THE WAY TO SHIGA, RIGHT?
YOU GUYS AREN'T STILL ON BAD TERMS AFTER ALL THAT, ARE YOU?!
I MEAN, SERI-NUMA-SAN SEEMS PRETTY DOWN...
DID SOME-THING HAPPEN? IS THAT WHAT YOU WANTED TO TALK ABOUT?
UH... NOTHING HAPPENED... ER... WHICH I GUESS IS KINDA THE PROBLEM...
HUH?
UH...

ズバーン
BOOM
WHAT WOULD YOU SAY ABOUT A GUY WHO GETS A HOTEL ROOM WITH A GIRL AND DOESN'T DO ANYTHING ?!
ブ
PTOO!
?!

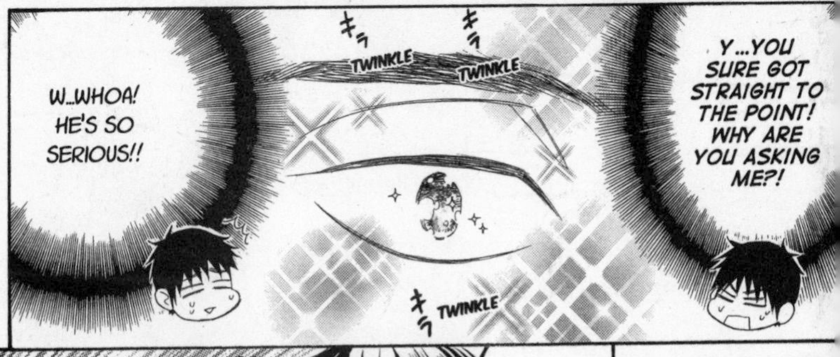
Y...YOU SURE GOT STRAIGHT TO THE POINT! WHY ARE YOU ASKING ME?!
キラ
TWINKLE
キラ
TWINKLE
キラ
TWINKLE
W...WHOA! HE'S SO SERIOUS!!

UH... WELL... I MEAN... LET'S SEE...
モゴモゴ
MUMBLE MUMBLE
BE HONEST !!
I'D SAY HE'S A COWARD !!
ズバ
ON THE MARK
COWARD
SHUNK
NGH ...!

YEAH ...
YEAH...
FIDGET
FIDGET
...

I MEAN... THINGS STARTED OFF ON THE RIGHT FOOT...
AND WE GOT INTO BED TOGETHER, BUT...
GRN
GRN
THEN I SAID, "YOU MUST BE TIRED. GOOD NIGHT."
AND ENDED UP GOING TO SLEEP ...

WHAT THE HECK? THAT'S THE WORST !!
You totally backed out, huh?
I KNOW.

WELL, WHY DON'T YOU APOLO-GIZE?
Be honest with her.
W-WELL, YEAH, BUT...
HUH? WHAT NOW?
WELL... TO BE PER-FECTLY HONEST ...

I DIDN'T KNOW WHAT TO DO...

UH, SO YOU MEAN... YOU DIDN'T KNOW HOW?
LIKE, HOW TO DO IT?
こくり
NOD
I SEE...
IGARASHI-KUN!!
ガ
GRAB
ッ

YOU SEEM TO KNOW A LOT ABOUT THIS STUFF...
PLEASE TEACH ME, IGARASHI-KUN!!

WHAAAA?!!
TELL ME YOU'RE JOKING!
キーンコーンカーンコーン…
DING
DONG
DANG
DONG
Asuma Mutsumi
I have stuff to do today, so I'm gonna head home first.
SORRY!
THERE. I SENT IT...

PING
Asuma Mutsumi
See you tomorrow.
I LOVE YOU
LOVE

PING
Asuma Mutsumi
I see. I also have stuff to do. Sorry. See you tomorrow.

Wow! HE SAID HE LOVES YOU!
Let's drop by there!
SEE THAT? EVERY-THING'S FINE!
See ya later!
THAT'S ...
I LOVE YOU
...WHAT SENPAI SAYS...
BUT...
MUTTER...
THIS WOULD NEVER HAPPEN IN A BL MANGA...

FOR GOD'S SAKE !!
BAM

WHY IS BL THE STAN-DARD YOU COM-PARE EVERY-THING TO?!
THIS IS YOU AND SENPAI WE'RE TALKING ABOUT!!

A...AH-CHAN...
I MEAN, THERE ARE PLENTY OF OTHER THINGS BESIDES BL TO COMPARE THIS TO, Y'KNOW!
Even in fiction!
OTHER THINGS ?

MUTSU-MI-SENPAI... AND ME...
GASP

TH... THAT'S RIGHT !!
HUH ?
UH, WHA ?!
CLATTER

WE'RE A STRAIGHT COUPLE, SO IF I'M COMPARING US TO SOMETHING, IT SHOULD BE A LOVEY-DOVEY SHOJO MANGA!!
HUH...? WHAT ?!

I'M GONNA CHECK 'EM OUT!!
だぁーっ
DASH
HEY, HOLD ON!
WHAT DO YOU MEAN BY THAT ?!
Mean-while...
AND SO...
THAT'S WHY I'VE BROUGHT YOU ALL HERE!!

BOOM
I STILL DON'T GET WHY YOU GATHERED US HERE!!

BESIDES, I DIDN'T WANT TO HEAR THAT STUFF...
WHY DO WE OF ALL PEO-PLE ...?
SHUT UP! YOU GUYS ARE IN THIS WITH ME!!
SOB...
YOU'RE AWFUL!

ANYWAY, I WANT US TO GIVE MUTSUMI-SAN SOME ADVICE!

Namely...
ON THE WAYS OF GETTING FRISKY!!
BOOM!
THE "HOW-TO" OF SEX!!

CAN'T HE JUST READ A SELF-HELP BOOK ON THAT...?
They have stuff like that on the Internet...

BUT PERSONAL STORIES ARE MORE HELPFUL THAN A MANUAL, RIGHT?
HUH?!

くあっ
ARGH
WHY ARE YOU ASKING ME? I HAVEN'T EVEN HAD MY FIRST KISS YET!!
YOU HAVE NO TACT, IGARASHI-SENPAI!!
YOU'RE TERRIBLE!!
わあっ
SOB
Now look what you did!
You made him cry!
SORRY, SHINO. I'M AWARE. IT'S JUST THAT NO ONE'S AT YOUR HOUSE, SO IT WAS CONVENIENT TO HOLD THE MEETING HERE.
YOU MONSTER!!
NANA, DO YOU HAVE ANY ADVICE?
HUH?
C'MON, WHY DO I HAVE TO TALK ABOUT THAT STUFF?
じ…っ
STARE...
URK!
Help me...
Help me...
I MEAN, STUFF LIKE THAT DEPENDS ON THE MOOD OF THE SITUATION...
AND I GUESS YOU CAN SAY YOUR INSTINCTS TAKE CARE OF THE REST...
ギッ
CREAK

KATHUD
AHHHHH!!
IDIOTS!! HOW AM I SUPPOSED TO TEACH SOMETHING I KNOW NOTHING ABOUT?!
KILL ME! JUST KILL ME ALREADY!!
Shenpai!
I HAD A FEEL-ING...
FLAIL
FLAIL
FLAIL
FLAIL
FLAIL
A man of many missed opportunities.

STARE
GASP
UH...
WHA?

TEACH US, MASTER IGA-RASHI!!
AW, MAN... I HAD A FEELING THIS WAS GONNA HAPPEN...
SHAKE
SHAKE
Plan back-fired.
I GUESS IT COMES DOWN TO ME!!
OKAY, GATHER 'ROUND, YOU VIRGINS!!
WOOO
WOOO
MASTER!!

And so, the boys ...
OH! OH! WHEN DO THE CLOTHES COME OFF?!
YES!
ME!
PICK ME!
YES!
ME!
OH! OH! IS IT A TURN OFF TO KISS WITH TONGUE AT THE START?!
YES!
ME!
ME!
ME!
OVER HERE!
ME TOO!
I'VE GOT ONE!
SHADDUP!
ME!
THAT STUFF DEPENDS ON THE MOOD OF THE SITUATION, AND HOW SHE RESPONDS.
WE DON'T UNDERSTAND! SHOW US WHAT YOU MEAN, MASTER!!
RAWR
HUH?
...pay unusually close attention to the crash course!!
STARE
I see...
I see...
...
Er...
It's gonna happen
Eek!
Mean-while, Kae...
BOOM
EURE-KA!

MY EYES HAVE BEEN OPENED ...!!
TWIRL
くるん
TWIRL
くるん
OH!! AH-CHAN?! I'VE FIGURED IT OUT! I UNDERSTAND NOW!!
HUH? UNDERSTAND WHAT?
インターネット
MANGA CAFE
24H

I READ A LOT OF ROMANTIC SHOJO MANGA!
YAY YAY
わくわく
IT WAS SO MUCH FUN!!
MY HEART WAS POUNDING!!
SOB SOB
うぉっうぉっ
THERE WERE MOMENTS WHERE I BAWLED MY EYES OUT...
WHIMPER
AND MOMENTS SO CUTE THAT I COULD DIE. IT WAS SO NEW!
SIIIGH
はああん
UH... UH-HUH.
AND Y'KNOW WHAT?

BOOM
ONE MANGA TOOK 20 VOLUMES FOR THE COUPLE TO KISS!!
HUH?
AND OTHERS TOOK ABOUT 10 VOLUMES... AND SOME WENT A YEAR WHERE NOTHING HAPPENS!!
OH, BUT STUFF HAPPENED PRETTY QUICKLY FOR THE MORE EXTREME ONES...
EEEK!
SIGH ...
SO... WHAT'S YOUR POINT?

SO WE JUST HAVE TO GO AT OUR OWN PACE, TOO!
OH.
UH, YEAH.
AND Y'KNOW WHAT ELSE?
HM?

I GET IT NOW.
GUYS ARE NO DIFFER-ENT...

JUST LIKE HOW NER-VOUS I WAS ...
...AND HOW MY HEART WAS RACING SO MUCH I COULDN'T THINK STRAIGHT ...
IT'S NO DIFFERENT FOR GUYS!
IT'S NORMAL FOR THINGS NOT TO GO SMOOTHLY.
TOTALLY NORMAL!
KAE-CHAN...!

I'VE ONLY SEEN REALLY AGGRES-SIVE MALE LEADS, SO I HAD NO IDEA!!
AH... YEAH? UH-HUH?
You're still on about that?
ANY-WAY...
MUTSUMI-SENPAI TOLD YOU THAT HE LOVES YOU, SO TRUST IN HIM!
HE'S A GOOD GUY!

YEAH!!

HER LOGIC IS ALL OVER THE PLACE, BUT SHE CAME TO THE RIGHT CONCLU-SION...
Whew, honestly.
CLASSIC KAE-CHAN...

THAT'S EVERY-THING!
OKAY ?!
YES, SIR!!
THANK YOU, MASTER !!
THAT WAS VERY EDUCA-TIONAL, MASTER!!
YOU ARE TRULY THE MASTER !!
WOOHOO!!
HON-ESTLY, CUT IT OUT!
OH, MU-TSUMI-SEN-PAI...
ONE LAST THING.
JUST REMEMBER NOT TO DO ANYTHING SHE DOESN'T WANT TO, AND IT'LL BE FINE. AND...
I think.
ALSO!
POINT
YOU SHOULD APOLOGIZE FOR FALLING ASLEEP !!
SHE MIGHT FEEL LIKE SHE WAS THE REASON.
FWIP
YEAH.

I'LL MAKE SURE TO DO THAT!
THANKS!
SLAM
WHAT AM I DOING ...?
は SIGH
YOU HAD NO OTHER CHOICE. IT IS MUTSUMI-SENPAI, AFTER ALL...
YEAH.
YOU CAN'T HELP BUT GET YOURSELF INVOLVED, CAN YOU?
I'm gonna make dinner. You wanna stay and eat?
SHUT UP!
And yeah, I'll eat..
YEAH ...
IT'S GONNA BE OKAY ...
FIRST, I'M GONNA TELL HER...

TMP
TMP
TMP
TMP
TMP
...HOW I FEEL.
MUTSUMI-SENPAI!!
SERI-NUMA-SAN!!

I WAS HEADING OVER TO SEE YOU.
CHATTER
M...ME, TOO...
CHATTER
CHATTER
読書週間

HEY...
I NEED TO TELL YOU SOME-THING, SERINUMA-SAN.

I'M SORRY THAT I FELL ASLEEP THAT DAY.
I REALLY REGRET IT. I DON'T KNOW WHAT I WAS DOING ...
I KNOW IT'S PATHETIC, BUT I GOT SCARED.
BUT ...
I REALLY DID WANT TO HANG OUT WITH YOU. THAT'S THE TRUTH.
I... I...
I WAS JUST HAPPY THAT WE COULD BE TOGETHER!

LET'S TAKE OUR TIME WITH THIS RELATION-SHIP.
WE DON'T HAVE TO RUSH.
AS LONG AS WE'RE TOGETHER, WE'LL HAVE ANOTHER CHANCE!
ANOTHER CHANCE ...
GASP
は っ!!
UH!
ER!
I DIDN'T MEAN IT LIKE THAT, UH...
BLUSH
BLUSH
I MEAN, CHANCE, AS IN, LIKE, FOR ME...
UHH, NEVER MIND... I, UH... I'M BEING WEIRD, AREN'T I...?!
YANK
HUH ?
AH!
?!
RATTLE
図書室
gn: Library

TMP
BADUMP
ドキン
BADUMP
ドキン
SERI-NUMA-SAN...
I LOVE YOU.
ドキン
BADUM
I LOVE YOU, TOO...!
ドキン
BADUMP

YEAH.
THERE'S NO NEED TO RUSH.
BE-CAUSE...
WE'LL ALWAYS BE TOGETHER, NOW AND FOREVER...

#53 TOGETHER FOREVER

Mornin'!
Morning!
CHATTER
ザワ
CHATTER
ザワ

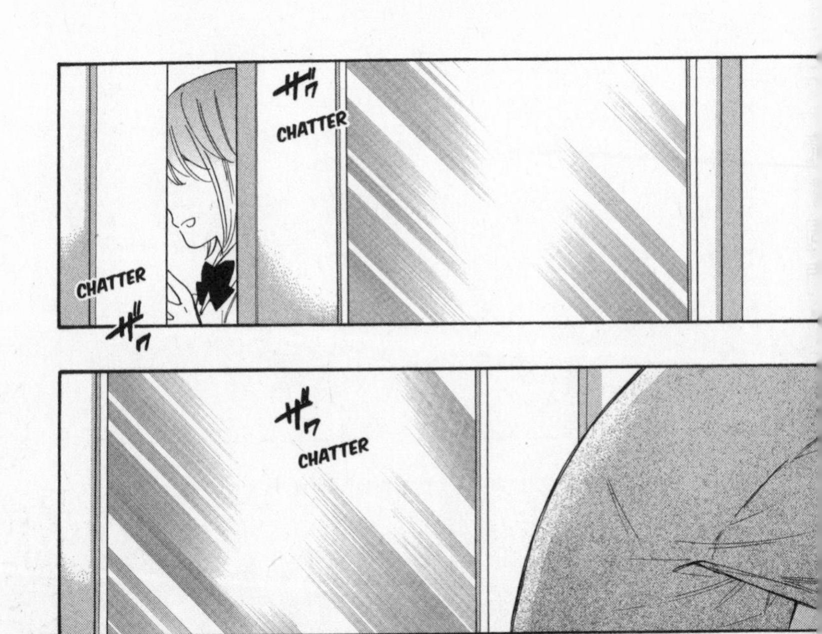
ザワ
CHATTER
ザワ
CHATTER
ザワ
CHATTER

CHATTER
ザワ
CHATTER
ザワ

CHATTER
ザワ

CHATTER
CHATTER
CHATTER

JOLT
?!

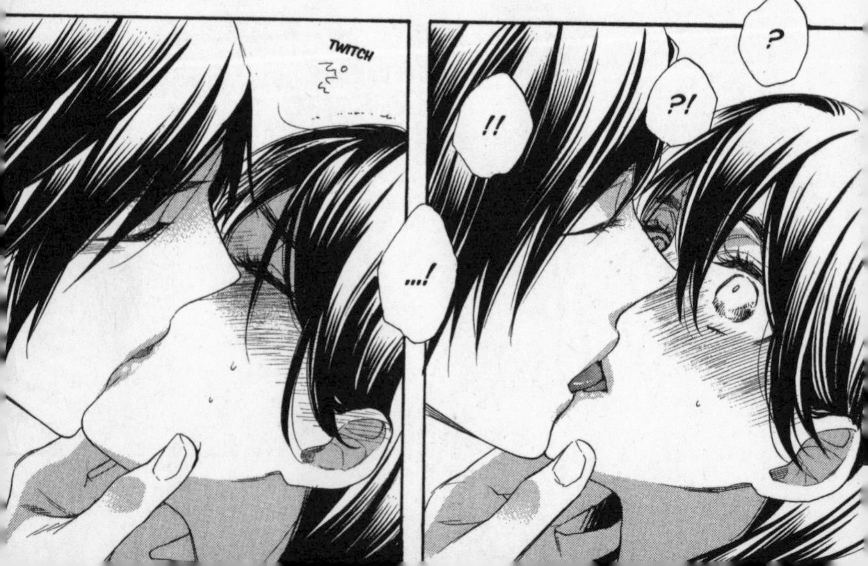
?
?!
!!
...!
TWITCH

CLATTER...
ガタッ
DING
キーン
DONG
コーン
JUMP
ぱっ
DONG
コーン
DANG
カーン
OH.
DING
キン
DONG
コン
DANG
カン
DONG
コン♪
HEH.
HEH HEH HEH!
BLUSH
SH... SHALL WE?!
UH, YEAH.

HOO BOY ...
I WILL PASS AROUND THE HAND-OUTS NOW.
I GOT REALLY INTO IT...
ぽわぁ～ん
FLUSHED
SEN-PAI...
...IS QUITE AG-GRES-SIVE...
TH...
THAT WAS ...
THAT WAS AMAZ-ING...

SO AMA-ZING ...
TWITCH

!!
NNNN-NNNGH !!
THUD
UH, UM, THE HAND-OUT...
ビクッ
JOLT
I'LL JUST LEAVE IT THERE ...

ぴら
FWIP
進路調査票
Post-secondary Survey
年 組 番
氏名

HM?

THE FALL... OF OUR SECOND YEAR...?
HM?
WHAT? IS SOME-THING WRONG?

IT'S THAT TIME!
WE ARE IN THE FALL OF OUR SECOND YEAR, AFTER ALL.
たはー SIGH
I GOTTA START THINKING ABOUT MY LIFE GOALS.

IT'S JUST...
HAZE
HAZE
MY MEMORY IS ALL JUMBLED ...
I GUESS ...
HAZE
WHA?
KAE-CHAN? ARE YOU OKAY?
...
KABOOM
?!
JOLT

Kae decided not to think about it!!
HEH HEH HEH
AH, WHAT-EVER!!

POST-SECOND-ARY PLANS, HUH... I'VE NEVER THOUGHT ABOUT IT...
YEAH ...
AND SOON, THE THIRD YEARS ARE GONNA GRADU-ATE, TOO...
YEAH! GRADU-ATE... GRADU-ATE...

COME TO THINK OF IT, WHAT IS MUTSUMI-SENPAI GOING TO DO AFTER HE GRADUATES?
GRADUATE?

THE THIRD-YEAR STUDENTS WILL GRADUATE.
THAT GOES WITHOUT SAYING.
SO, UH, THAT MEANS...
MUTSUMI-SENPAI...

HUH..? I FEEL LIKE MY MEMORY IS ALL JUMBLED...
ME, TOO... HUH?

HOW ...
HOW COULD I FORGET ?!
TICK

3 - B
I GOT CARRIED AWAY...
I HOPE I DIDN'T TURN HER OFF...
THUD
THUD
THUD
THUD
SHENPAIIIII!!
!!!
BOLT
SHENPAI SHENPAI SHENPAI SHENPAI !!
BOOM
HUH?! SERI-NUMA-SA...
DON'T GRADU-ATE!!
AGH!
HER AGAIN?
DOES SHE EVER ENTER THE CLASSROOM NORMALLY?
WHAT IS IT TO-DAY?
WAAHHH!!
HUH ?!

WAAHHH!
S... SERI-NUMA-SAN... HOW 'BOUT WE GO SOME-WHERE PRIVATE?!
GULP
IS MUTSU-MI REALLY OKAY WITH A GIRL LIKE HER...?
SOB
CHOMP
SOB
CHOMP

Wrapper: Bread with Jam, Stawberry

DOES IT TASTE GOOD?
YESH.
HAVE YOU CALMED DOWN?
YESH.
CHOMP
CHOMP
CHOMP
Taming with food
THAT'S GOOD TO HEAR.
S...SENPAI... I WAS THINKING...
YEAH?

WHY DON'T YOU STAY BACK A YEAR?
AND THEN WE CAN GRADUATE TOGETHER NEXT YEAR!!
NICE IDEA!!
WHAT DO YOU SAY?!
OH, SHE'S STILL IN THE THICK OF IT.

NOW, NOW. YOU WANT ANOTHER PASTRY?
Here! The next one has cream filling!
YESH.

GRADUATION...
YEAH...
I'M GONNA HAVE TO GRADUATE HIGH SCHOOL.
U...UNTIL TODAY... I...I KEPT THINKING WE'D BE IN SCHOOL TOGETHER FOREVER...
SNIFF
TO BE HONEST, I FELT THE SAME WAY...
I WONDER WHY.
YEAH...

HEH HEH ...
HOW STRANGE.
YEAH, IT SURE IS!
EVEN IF YOU GRA-DU-ATE ...
WE CAN STILL SEE EACH OTHER, RIGHT?
IT'S NOT LIKE YOU'LL BE FAR, FAR AWAY.
I'M SAD THAT YOU'LL BE GONE, SENPAI, BUT...
I GUESS I KINDA LOST IT BACK THERE.
I'M SORRY.
DON'T BE.
SQUEEZE
I'M SAD, TOO.
BUT TO BE HONEST, SERINUMA-SAN, I'M GLAD TO HEAR...
...THAT YOU FEEL THAT WAY.

どっきゅん♡
BADUMP
SHEN-PAI...
S...SINCE YOU'LL BE GRADUATING, I WANT TO MAKE MORE MEMORIES TOGETHER BEFORE THEN!
WE GOTTA !!
YEAH.
OKAY! THEN AS SOON AS SCHOOL'S OUT, WE'LL GO SOME-WHERE AND...
HOW 'BOUT NOW?
HUH?

RIGHT HERE.
WHY NOT MAKE A MEMORY OF YOU BEING RIGHT HERE...
コツッ
TMP
...WITH ME?

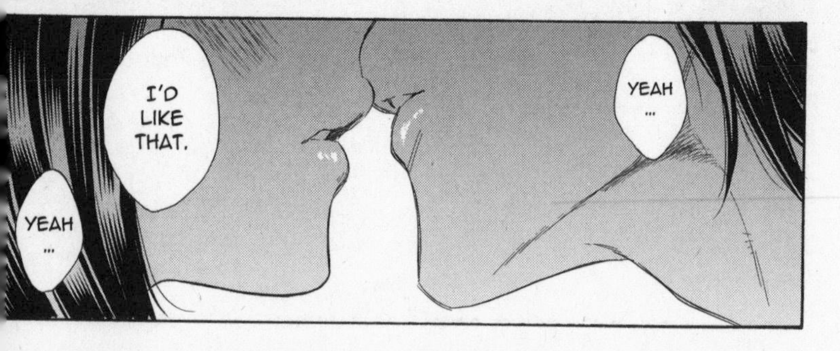
YEAH ...
I'D LIKE THAT.
YEAH ...

...
TWITCH
ぴくん
MM
...

キーン
DING
コーン
DONG
カーン
DANG
コーン
DONG
はっ
GASP

THERE'S THE BELL AGAIN...
HEH HEH.
HA HA.

WE MADE A MEMORY. ♡
YEAH.

I WANT TO MAKE MORE...
MORE ...
MEM-ORIES ...

MEMORIES OF JUST US TWO...

MANY MORE OF THEM...

I FEEL LIKE IT'S SO RARE TO SEE A CAT AT SCHOOL!
IT'S A CALICO, SO I GUESS IT'S A GIRL?
SHE'S SO CUTE.
I LOVE CATS, BUT MY BROTHER HAS A CAT ALLERGY, SO...
HUH? IS THAT SO?
WELL... IN THAT CASE...
...WANNA COME OVER AND MEET MY CAT?
HUH...?
GASP

M...
MEANING...
ドキン
BADUMP
HUH...?
SENPAI'S PLACE...?
D...
ドキン
BADUMP
ドキン
BADUMP
...DOES THAT MEAN...?
Am I overthinking it? Am I overthinking it?!
UH...
BOOM
YOU DON'T WANT TO...?

TH...THANKS FOR INVITING ME OVER...!
HOLD ON, LET ME GET US SOME TEA.
O... OKAY!
BADUMP
FIDGET
BADUMP
FIDGET
BADUMP
BADUMP

BADUMP
BADUMP
BADUMP
N... NO ONE'S HERE ...
BADUMP
BADUMP
BADUMP
THIS IS...OUR CHANCE, RIGHT...?
TREMBLE
HEY!! THIS IS NO TIME TO BE TREMBLING !!
BESIDES, I'M WEARING CUTE UNDERWEAR TODAY!
I'VE COME THIS FAR, SO I'M NOT GONNA BACK OUT!!
HAH!
KNOCK
KNOCK
KNOCK
KER-CHAK
SORRY TO KEEP YOU WAITING.
HERE YOU GO.
UH, THANK YOU.
SILENCE
PURRR!

Uh, let's see...
PURRRR
CHACHA-CHAN IS ADOR-ABLE.
SHE'S SO FRIEND-LY.
CHACHA'S ACTUALLY PRETTY SHY AROUND NEW PEOPLE AND KEEPS HER DISTANCE FROM THEM, Y'KNOW...
HUH? REALLY?
YEAH.
IT LOOKS LIKE CHACHA LIKES YOU, TOO, SERINUMA-SAN.
BADUMP

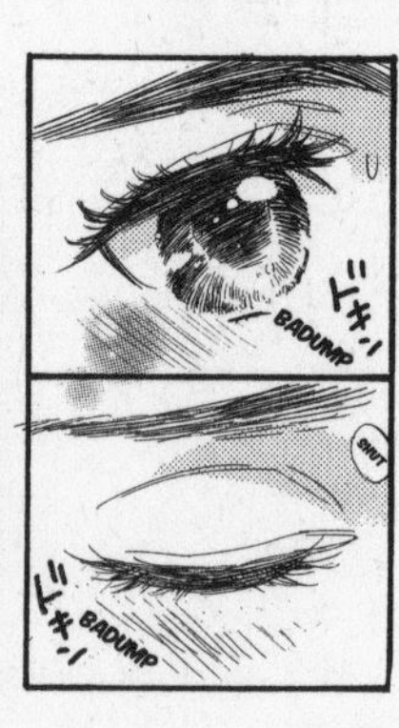
BADUMP
SHUT
BADUMP

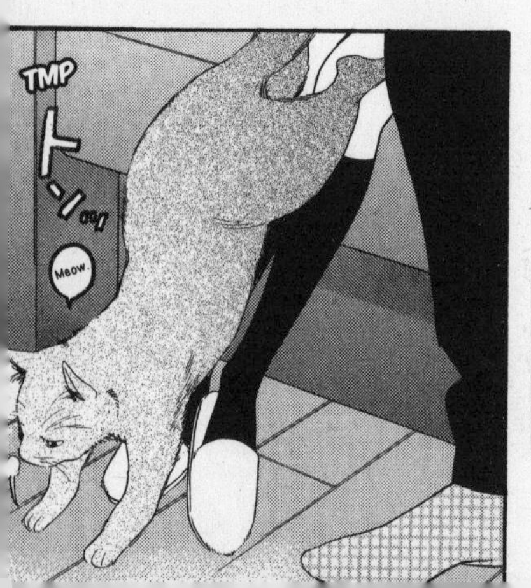
TMP
Meow.

SQUEEZE
CREAK
KISS
KISS
JOLT
OH...!

I'M HOME !!
YOU HERE, ASUMA ?!
BAM
?!

OH.

BLUSH
あ あ
...
あ
KRIKT
KRIKT
Soul crushing
MY BAD, MY BAD! I'LL STEP OUT!
UH, SHOULD I COME BACK IN AN HOUR?!
Longer?
HEH
HEH

DON WOR ABOU IT!
I'LL SEE YOU LATER!
HUH ?
S... SERI-NUMA-SA...
IT'S OKAY! DON'T COME ANY CLOSER !!
WHAT ARE YOU DOING HERE, KAZUMA ...?
My bad!
NOTH-ING! I JUST SUD-DENLY GOT HOME-SICK.
SO SORRY, MAN!
YEAH... LET ME PUNCH YOU...
HUH? NO!!

THUD
H...
HOW CAN THIS HAP-PEN ?!
W
A
A
A
H
H
H
THIS WAS A CHANCE THAT WOULDN'T COME AGAIN!
THAT DEVIL !!!!

I CAN'T LEAVE THINGS LIKE THIS!
I'M HOME!
IF THIS IS HOW IT'S GONNA BE...
KER-CHAK
ガチャ
I'M GONNA TAKE MATTERS INTO MY OWN HANDS!
MY MOM AND BROTHER ARE ALWAYS AT HOME, BUT...
OH, ELCOME HOME, KAE.
I'VE GOTTA SOMEHOW KICK THEM OUT OF THE HOUSE FOR A DAY!!
YOU CAME HOME AT JUST THE RIGHT TIME. I NEED TO LET YOU KNOW...
THIS WEEKEND, MY FRIEND INVITED ME TO A FANCY HOTEL AND SPA FOR A ONE NIGHT STAY...
UFUFU...
AND 'LL BE OING ON A ETREAT TO AGANO ITH MY CLUB.

ARE YOU ALL RIGHT HAVING THE HOUSE TO YOUR-SELF ALL WEEKEND?

HEH...
?
HEH HEH ...
OH...
WOBBLE...

JUST LEAVE IT TO ME!
YOU TWO HAVE FUN!
SMILE
THIS IS IT!!!

THE HEAVENS ...
THE HEAVENS HAVE BLESSED US...!!
MUTSUMI-SENPAI!!
OH...

SERI-NUMA-SAN!
I'M REALLY SORRY ABOUT YESTER-DAY...!
NO, DON'T BE!
YOU COULDN'T HELP IT. IT WAS THAT EVIL, UH... I MEAN, KAZUMA-SAN.
MORE IMPOR-TANTLY ...
SENPAI.
きゅ
TUG
TH...
THIS SATUR-DAY...
WOULD YOU LIKE TO COME OVER TO MY HOUSE...?
N...
NO ONE WILL BE HOME THIS WEEKEND...

OH.
MU-TSUMI!

JUST THE PERSON I WANT TO SEE.
DO YOU HAVE A MOMENT TO TALK?
UH, SURE.

ANY-WAY...
職員室
THIS IS IMPOR-TANT, SO...
GIVE IT SOME SERIOUS THOUGHT.
ALL RIGHT.

Sign: Staff Room

PERSON-
ALLY, I
RECOM-
MEND
YOU GO
FOR IT.

RATTLE
ガララ
EXCUSE
ME.

TMP...
...

That Saturday...
ALL RIGHT!!
MY MOM AND BROTHER ARE OUT OF THE HOUSE!!
MY ROOM...
...IS ALL CLEANED UP!!
PERFECT!!
WHEW
THE HOUSE IS ALL READY FOR SENPAI!!
HE'S GONN BE HERE SOO...
IT'LL BE FINE. IT'LL BE FINE.
BADUMP
BADUMP
BADUMP
BADUMP
JUST RELAX...!
BADUMP
BADUMP
DING DONG
JOLT
EEK!
THUD THUD THUD
ONE MOMENT!!
COMING!!

OH.
HELLO.
CAN I COME IN?
MU-TSUMI-SENPAI!
WEL-COME!

HERE, I BROUGHT A GIFT...
WOW! THANK YOU SO MUCH!

SLAM
OH, I PREPARED US SOME DINNER!
AL-THOUGH IT'S JUST CURRY.
Heh heh heh!
REALLY? I'M LOOKING FORWARD TO IT!
THANK YOU!

HAVE SOME TEA.
THANKS.
CLINK

HEH HEH HEH.
I.. I'LL JUST SCOOCH NEXT TO YOU.
SCUTTLE
...

?
GLANCE

SENPAI... SEEMS SO CALM.
EVEN THOUGH I FEEL LIKE I'M ABOUT TO BURST...
I WONDER WHAT HE'S THINKING ABOUT...
I WANT HIM TO LOOK THIS WAY...

LOOK AT ME ...
H...
HERE GOES!
FWUMP

UH...
GASP
はっ
SENPAI.
I LOVE YOU...

WAIT.

...
THE TRUTH IS...
THERE'S...
...SOMETHING I NEED TO TELL YOU FIRST.
R... RIGHT NOW?
HUH? WH... WHAT IS IT?
I FOUND OUT...
...THAT I GOT A RECOMMENDATION TO A UNIVERSITY.
WHAT ...?!
WOW! THAT'S AMAZING !!
WOW !!
EEK!
THAT'S GREAT, MUTSUMI-SENPAI! I MEAN, YOU DO HAVE REALLY GOOD MARKS!
THE SCHOOL ...

...IS IN
KYOTO.

HUH...?

#54 SENPAI'S DREAM

KYOTO?

...
UH...
WHAT ...
...DO YOU MEAN?
HUH ...?

BUT THAT'S.. FAR AWAY...
KYOTO'S FAR AWAY, ISN'T IT?
YEAH.
W...WE WON'T BE ABLE TO SEE EACH OTHER WHEN WE WANT TO...
W...WE WON'T BE ABLE TO HOLD HANDS WHEN WE WANT TO!!
YEAH.

UH, BUT IT'S JUST UNDER THREE HOURS AWAY BY BULLET TRAIN.
ACK!
BUT THE BULLET TRAIN IS SO EXPEN-SIVE!!
UH, RIGHT.

...!!
S-SERI-NUMA-SAN...
TREMBLE
TREMBLE
H...

HAVE YOU AL-READY MADE YOUR DECI-SION?
WITHOUT EVEN TELLING ME...?
ス
FWIP
NO...I HAVEN'T DECIDED ANY-THING.
THAT'S WHY I'M TELLING YOU NOW.
SO...?
I...
I WANT TO GO.
THERE'S A PROFESSOR I REALLY ADMIRE.

B...BUT THEN, WE'LL BE SEPARAT-ED.
CLENCH...
SENPAI, ARE YOU REALLY OKAY WITH THAT...?!
IF YOU...
...CAN FORGIVE ME...
THAT'S ...
THAT'S SO...
...UN-FAIR OF YOU...
IF YOU PUT IT THAT WAY, I...I...

KAPOW
I'M DEFINITELY NOT GONNA FORGIVE YOU!!
WHAM
CLATTER
JOLT

BWAHHHH!!
OF COURSE I'M NOT FINE WITH THIS!!
WE'RE GONNA BE APART!!
IF WE'RE APART, SOMEBODY...
S... SOMEBODY MIGHT STEAL YOU AWAY!

SENPAI, YOU CAN BE SO CLUELESS THAT...
...SOMEONE LIKE YASHIRO-SENPAI WILL SNAP YOU UP BEFORE YOU KNOW IT!
You don't even notice when someone hits on you!
TH... THAT'S NOT TRUE.
YOU'RE THE ONLY ONE FOR ME, SERINUMA-SAN!
YOU DON'T KNOW THAT!!

BESIDES, UNIVERSITY IS WHERE GUYS AND GIRLS ON THE HUNT GET TOGETHER, BREAK UP, GET TOGETHER AGAIN, THEN SUDDENLY SHUFFLE PARTNERS AROUND LIKE SOME REALITY TV SHOW!!!
LOVEY DOVEY
LOVEY DOVEY
YEAHHH!
TENNIS IN THE SUMMER
SKIING AND SNOWBOARDING IN THE WINTER
YEAHHH!
*Kae's perception
JOINING A CLUB HERE, GOING OUT FOR DRINKS THERE, GOING TO MATCH-MAKING PARTIES EVERY NIGHT AND HAVING THE TIME OF THEIR LIVES!!
I...I THINK YOUR VIEW OF UNIVER-SITY IS PRETTY SKEWED!

AND YOU'LL BE GOIN ALL BY YOUR-SELF!!
URK
HURK
URK
...

YOU HAVE... THAT LITTLE FAITH IN ME?

UH...
FLUSTER
TH... THAT'S NOT WHAT I MEAN ...
WHAT I MEAN IS, UH...
LIKE, AREN'T YOU WORRIED ABOUT LEAVING ME ALL BY MYSELF?!

TO BE HONEST, YEAH. YOU'D GO NUTS RIGHT AWAY.
SAY WHAT ?!

ゆらっ
WOBBLE
YOU'RE WORRIED ABOUT ME, YET YOU'D STILL LEAVE ME BEHIND ...

HUH, UH...
I'VE HAD IT!! GO HOME!!
YOU JERK!
NOW !!

BEAT IT!
TOSS
WHOA
SERI-NUMA-SAN! LET'S TALK AGAIN WHEN YOU'VE CALMED DOWN!
SLAM
WE HAVE NOTHING TO TALK ABOUT!!

KER-CHAK
TMP
TMP
TMP
TMP
TMP
TMP

PLOD...
...!
SENPAI ...
YOU IDIOT ...!

2-A
BLOAT

Bag: Bread with Jam

I...
I'M NOT GONNA BE WON OVER SO EASILY!!
GOBBLE GOBBLE
...
K... KAE-CHAN?
WHAT HAP-PENED THIS TIME...?
BWOOSH
SPLATTER
FLINCH
TWINGE
AH-CHAN...
S... SENPAI... IS...
...GONNA DUMP MEEEE!
HUH?!
WAAAHHH

WHAT ?!
HE'S GOING TO UNIVERSITY IN KYOTO ?!

YEAH ...
AND HE'S GONNA LEAVE ME BEHIND ...

M... MUTSUMI-SENPAI IS DUMPING ME!!
URGH
URK
URGH
URK
Y... YOU'RE BEING DRAMATIC.
SO IT'S GONNA BE LONG DISTANCE!

BUT HE DIDN'T ASK YOU TO BREAK UP WITH HIM, DID HE?
No way...
N...NO...

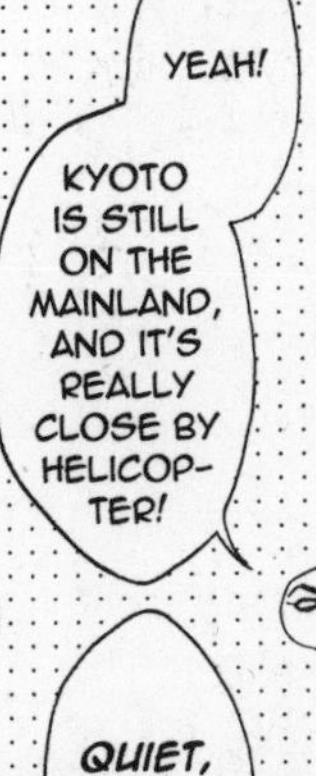
SO THERE'S STILL ROOM TO TALK THINGS OUT!!
YEAH!
KYOTO IS STILL ON THE MAINLAND, AND IT'S REALLY CLOSE BY HELICOPTER!

QUIET, YOU.

I KNOW IT MUST BE TOUGH FOR YOU, SERINUMA-SAN, BUT...

...IF I GOT RECOMMENDED TO A SCHOOL WITH A COACH I WANTED TO TRAIN WITH, I THINK I'D WANNA GO, TOO.
YOU CAN'T ASK HIM TO GIVE UP ON HIS DREAM JUST LIKE THAT.

"DREAM"...
BADUMP...
BOOM
NO WAY!!
IF IT WERE ME, I'D PICK THE GIRL!!
ME, TOO!!
RIGHT?!
YEAH!
THOSE TWO IDIOTS JUST HAD TO PIPE UP AGAIN...

I CAN'T JUST SIT BACK AND WATCH!!! I'M GONNA GO TALK TO MUTSUMI-SENPAI!!
I'M GOING, TOO!!
WHAAA ?!

HEY! DON'T, YOU GUYS!
SLAM
AGH ...

HONESTL THOSE TWO ARE CUT FRO THE SAM CLOTH.
What do you think? Nana x Shino? Or Shino x Nana?
Mmm, I'd say Shino x Nana.
SERI-NUMA-SAN...
YOU KNOW ...
I THIN IT'D BE GOOD IF YO THOUG ABOUT
...WHAT YOU WOUL DO...
...IF YOU HAD A DREAM YOU WANTED SO BADLY TO FULFILL.

WE HEARD YOU GOT RECOMMENDED TO A UNIVERSITY IN KYOTO ...
ARE YOU SERIOUS ABOUT GOING?!
YEAH.
I AM.
BOOM
HUHHHH?!
I DON'T GET YOU AT ALL!!
IF IT WERE ME, I'D STAY!!
BOOM
YOU CAN STUDY ANYWHERE, Y'KNOW!
BUT YOU ONLY HAVE A GIRLFRIEND HERE!
AND YOU CAN'T GO LONG DISTANCE!
'CAUSE THEN YOU CAN'T TOUCH EACH OTHER!!
RIGHT?!
HONKA
HONKA
HONKA
HONKA
HOW VULGAR.
UH ...

INSTEAD OF GOING ABROAD WITH MY PARENTS, I STAYED IN JAPAN SO I COULD BE WITH YOU ALL.
YOU DON'T FEEL THE SAME WAY, MUTSUMI-SENPAI ...?
...
HERE ...
Travel Through History
FWI
I'VE LIKED CASTLES SINCE I WAS LITTLE...
'Cause they're cool...
I GREW INTERESTED IN HISTORY AFTER READING THIS BOOK.
I'VE READ ALL OF THE WRITINGS BY THIS PROFES-SOR.
AND THIS PROFESSO TEACHES AT THE SCHOOL I WANT TO GO TO.
SO...
THIS IS MORE IMPOR-TANT THAN SERI-NUMA?

I CAN'T COMPARE THE TWO.
BESIDES, I DON'T INTEND ON BREAKING UP WITH SERINUMA-SAN.
I BELIEVE WE'LL BE OKAY...
'CAUSE OUR HEARTS ARE CONNECTED.
WHAT'S THE POINT IF YOU'RE THE ONLY ONE WHO BELIEVES THAT?
DON'T YOU GET WHAT IT IS THAT BOTHERS SERINUMA?!

IF YOU TELL HER TO TRUST IN SOME-THING SHE CAN'T SEE, OF COURSE SHE'LL FEEL ANXIOUS!!
IF YOU WANT HER TO TRUST IN YOU, WHY NOT GIVE HER SOMETHING, ANYTHING, THAT'LL SERVE AS PROOF?!
NANA-SHIMA-SHENPAI... YOU'RE SO COOL!!
Oh my god...
He actually sounds respect-able!!
IF...
...YOU'RE GONNA KEEP SAYING STUPID STUFF...
BOOM
I'M GONNA TAKE SERINUMA FOR MYSELF!! THIS IS MY SHOT, MAN!
HA HA HA HA HA!!
TAKE THAT! HEH!
AND HE RUINED IT!!

ANYWAY, THAT'S ALL!!
TOO-DLES!!
SHWOOP
SLAM
JEEZ...
HEY, WAI...
...
PROOF...?
BADUMP

MU-TSUMI-SENPAI...
HUH?
DO YOU MIND IF I BORROW THIS?
...

"A DREAM"
...

IF I... HAD A DREAM ...?

くあッ
ARGH!
NO WAY!!
IF IT WERE ME, I'D TOTALLY PICK MUTSUMI-SENPAI!!
NO MATTER HOW MANY TIMES I MULL IT OVER, THAT'S A GIVEN!!

IT'S TRUE THAT I DON'T HAVE A SPECIFIC DREAM YET!
BUT I'D BE INTERESTED IN, WELL, RESEARCH ON PHYSICALLY JOINING THE 2-D WORLD!!
AND I STILL WOULDN'T WANT TO BE SEPARATED FROM MUTSUMI-SENPAI!!
HURRNG
URRG
BUT THIS IS ALL HYPOTHETICAL, SO MAYBE I'M STILL NOT TAKING IT SERIOUSLY ENOUGH?!
OKAY, BUT EVEN SO!
MUMBLE MUMBLE MUMBLE MUMBLE MUMBLE MUMBLE MUMBLE MUMBLE MUMBLE MUMBLE MUMBLE
SERI-NUMA-SENPAI.
DO YOU HAVE A MINUTE?
SHINO-MIYA-KUN?
UH, COULD YOU...
...TAKE A LOOK AT THIS?
A BOOK?
IT'S SO WORN OUT...

IT BELONGS TO MUTSUMI SENPAI.
HE SAID THIS WAS THE BOOK THAT GOT HIM INTO HISTORY.
IT'S INCREDIBLE HOW WORN OUT IT IS...

THIS BOO ...?
OH... SO THIS AUTHOR IS THE ONE...
"THERE'S A PROFES-SOR I ADMIRE."
HE BOOK-MARKED SO MANY OF THE PAGES...
HE REALLY LIKES THIS, HUH...?

A DREAM ...
TWINGE
ズキッ
UH ...

WHEN ...
...MY PARENTS WENT TO NORWAY...
WHOOSH
...I STAYED HERE...

...'CAUSE I WANTED TO BE WITH YOU, SERINUMA-SENPAI.

UH... AND ...
THE OTHER SENPAI, TOO.
HEH HEH ...
AT FIRST ...
MY PARENTS WERE TOTALLY AGAINST IT.

NATU-RALLY, THEY WERE WOR-RIED ABOUT ME.
I WAS IMMATURE AND CLUMSY...
BUT IN THE END, THEY AGREED TO LET ME STAY.
AND I THINK IT'S BECAUSE THEY TRUSTED ME.
...!
I MEAN, I'M SURE YOUR SITUATION WITH MUTSUMI-SENPAI IS TOTALLY DIFFERENT FROM MINE WITH MY PARENTS ...
B... BUT!
THEY LET ME GO, TRUSTING THAT I'D BE ALL RIGHT.
AND FOR THAT REASON ...
I FEEL LIKE... I'M TRYING MY BEST TO DO WELL ON MY OWN.

...!
UH, UM... I KNOW I STILL NEED A LOT OF HELP!
Like, around the house and stuff...
BUT I MEANT LIKE... IN MY OUT-LOOK ON LIFE! AND STUFF !!
UH, I'M SORRY.
I'M NOT GETTING MY POINT ACROSS VERY WELL!
SO... UH...

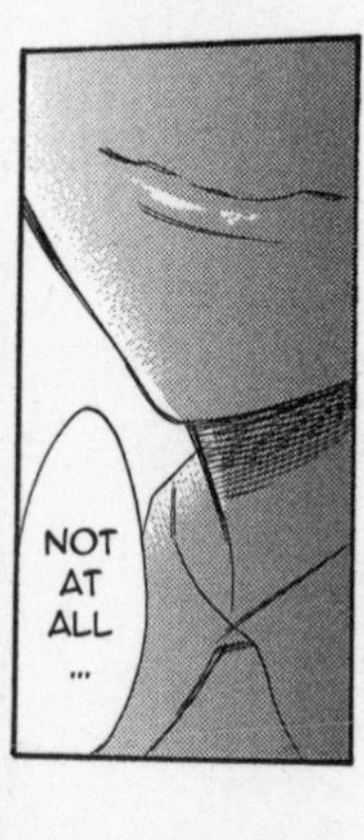
NOT AT ALL ...

I UNDER-STAND WHAT YOU'RE SAYING.
THANKS.
WHOOSH
BUT...
IT'S STILL NO USE.

WHEN I THINK ABOUT SENPAI GOING AWAY...
IT HURTS... I FEEL OVER-WHELMED WITH LONELINESS AND ANXIETY.
I CAN'T HELP BUT FEEL SO SCARED...!
I'M SO PATHETIC FOR FEELING THIS WAY...
B...
BUT ...
BUT–
SENPAI ...

AN-OTHER PAGE CREASED OPEN...
HE EVEN WROTE ON IT...

THE EDGES ARE ALL WORN OUT HERE...
HE MUST HAVE READ THIS PAGE A LOT, TOO...

SENPAI'S DREAM...
THIS BOOK IS PROOF OF IT.
TMP

I GET SO ANXIOUS ...

I DON'T KNOW WHAT TO DO...

I MEAN, THESE FEELINGS AREN'T TANGIBLE.

CLENCH
I'M... ONLY THINKING ABOUT MYSELF ...
I FEEL SO HELP-LESS.
I WANT TO DO SOME-THING ABOUT THIS...

PIIING

BUT WHAT?

23:30

GASP
"MIRAGE SAGA" IS ON.
DU-DUN
Mirage Saga

SHION!
WHERE ARE YOU GOING AT THIS HOUR OF THE NIGHT?

YOU'RE BEING SO FORMAL.

OR ARE YOU TOO EMBAR-RASSED TO SAY YOU'RE GOING AFTER HER?
FSH

NON-SENSE!
I'M HEADING NORTH.
IF I FOLLOW HER...
...SHE'LL LEAD ME TO *THE CLAWED MAN.*
SO LONG AS I'VE FOUND MY TARGET, I HAVE NO REASON TO JOIN YOUR GROUP.
THIS IS WHERE WE GO OUR SEPA-RATE WAYS.
FWIP
LIKE I SAID ...
...DON'T BE SO FORMAL...
HAH !!
GSHNK

SCREAK
ギッ
YOU WANT TO TAKE ME ON?
GRIN
ZSH
HOW NICE THAT YOU'VE FOUND YOUR FOE AT LAST...
...I LEND YOU THIS, AS A GIFT.

WHAT I ASK FOR
IN RETURN... IS YOUR SWORD, SHION.
HAND IT OVER.
YOU SAID YOU WANTED TO SEE THE END OF THE EARTH.
IF SO...
...YOU AND I SHARE THE SAME GOAL.
SO ONCE YOU GET YOUR REVENGE...
YOU SHOULD GO SEE IT YOURSELF.
REMEMBER
I'M LENDING THIS TO YOU.
SWEAR YOU'LL RETURN IT.
AND SO, SHION PARTED WAYS WITH TERRA.
HOWEVER, THEY WILL NOT BE PARTED FOREVER...

IF THEY CONTINUE TO CHASE THE SAME LIGHT...
...THEY WILL MEET AGAIN... AT THE ENDS OF THE EARTH.

"IF THEY CONTINUE TO CHASE THE SAME LIGHT" ...
...!!

はっ
GRAB

BRRING
BRRING

HELLO, SERI-NUMA-SAN?
OH, SENPAI ...!
THANKS FOR CALLING. ARE YOU FEELING BETTER NOW?
UH, YES ...
UH, SORRY ABOUT... THE LAST FEW DAYS.
I...
I'D LIKE TO HAVE A PROPER TALK...
...ABOUT WHERE THIS RELATION-SHIP IS GOING.
OKAY.
BUT BEFORE THAT, THERE'S JUST ONE REQUEST I'D LIKE TO MAKE.
WHAT'S THAT?

I...
I WANT TO SEE WITH MY OWN EYES... *WHERE* YOU'LL BE GOING TO SCHOOL, SENPAI.
SO...
...LET'S GO TO KYOTO TOGETHER!!

KiSS HiM, NOT ME!

#55 EVERYONE'S OWN JOURNEY

KiSS HiM,
NOT ME!

HUSTLE
ばた
BUSTLE
ばた
PANT
はっ
PANT
はっ
SENPAI!!

HEY, SERINUMA-SAN! OVER HERE!

SORRY FOR BEING LATE. I FORGOT SOMETHING AT MY HOUSE...
T-TEP
IT'S ALL RIGHT.
C'MON, LET'S GET ON.
OKAY!

パァーーン
WHOOSH
THE TRAIN IS NOW DEPARTING.
プルルルル…
DIIING DIIING

FWOOOSH

SORRY FOR SAYING I WANTED TO GO TO KYOTO ALL OF A SUDDEN ...

NO, NO.
I ALSO WANTED TO CHECK OUT THE PLACE, SO IT WORKED OUT WELL.
Have some tea.
Oh, thank you.
OH, I... I SEE.
BE-SIDES ...
I WAS HAPPY WHEN YOU SAID YOU WANTED TO GO SEE THE PLACE FIRST-HAND...
SENPAI ...
GULP

コオオオ
VWOOSH
OH.
MOUNT FUJI LOOKS SO PRETTY ...
オ

UH ...

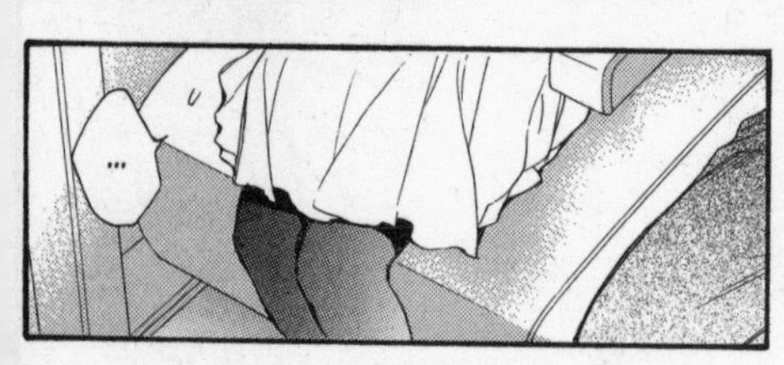
...

京都
きょうと
Kyōto
しんおおさか
Shin Ōsaka
京
まいばら
Maibara

CLACK

... SO THIS IS...
YEP, MY FIRST-CHOICE SCHOOL.

CHATTER CHATTER
WE'VE FINALLY ARRIVED ...
MHMM ...

IF THE SCHOOL IS HERE, YOU'LL BE LIVING SOME-WHERE NEARBY... RIGHT?
YEAH... I SUPPOSE SO.
RIGHT...

Sh...
SHOULD WE CHECK IT OUT ?!
HUH?
GULP
C'MON!
...

Cafe
OPEN

WHEW!!
THIS CAMPUS IS SO BIG!!
LOTS OF PEOPLE, TOO...
COMPARED TO OUR HIGH SCHOOL, YEAH.
YEAH.

IT REALLY IS...
... QUITE FAR...
YEAH...
I CAN'T ...
...COME VISIT YOU VERY EASILY AT THIS DISTANCE, HUH?
YEAH...
BUT...

...THIS IS WHERE YOUR DREAM IS, SENPAI.
I...

...FEEL LONELY.
I WONDER ABOUT WHAT'LL HAPPEN...
...IF WE'RE APART.
THAT'S ALL.
BUT THAT *DOES* REALLY SCARE ME.

SO...
PLIP
THAT'S WHY...
PLIP
I WANT YOU TO PROMISE ...
...THAT WE'LL STILL BE TOGETHER IN THE FUTURE, TOO.

OF COURSE !!
I UNDER-STAND.
I PROM-ISE.

GLARE!!
NO...!!
YOU DON'T UNDER-STAND.
FLINCH

THE... PROMISE I WANT YOU TO MAKE ME IS...
RUSTLE

婚姻届
Marriage Registration
平成 年 月
ばん
BOOM
THIS!!
?!
ばっ
THE PROMISE I WANT IS A MASSIVE ONE, Y'KNOW!!
I...I MEAN IT!!
ぶ
ぶわ
BLOOSH
HUH...?
...

BWAAAAHHH
WILL YOU SIGN YOUR NAME HERE?
CAN YOU ?!
NEVER MIND,
SIGN IIIIT !!!!
HA...
GA HA!
HA! HA! HA! HA!
WHAT ARE YOU LAUGHING AT?!
SHOCK
JUST LIKE I SAID...
YOU DO THE CRAZIEST THINGS, SERI-NUMA-SAN. I GET SO WORRIED!
HYUK!
RUSTLE
RUSTLE
WHAT?!

BUT...
...IT SEEMS LIKE WE'RE THINKING THE SAME THING.
HUH ...?
THIS IS...

...MY WAY OF ASKING YOU...
...TO STAY TOGETHER WITH ME FOREVER.
WILL YOU ACCEPT?
...
Y...
...ES.
YES...!

THIS IS MY PROMISE TO YOU.
LET'S BE TOGETHER ...

...FOREVER.

QUIVER
...!

ARE YOU SCARED?

...
P...PLEASE BE GENTLE WITH ME...

I FEEL THE SAME WAY.
BE GENTLE WITH ME, TOO, SERI-NUMA-SAN.

HA!
AHA!
HA! HA!
OKAY!
I WILL!

I LOVE YOU,
KAE.

SEN-PAI,
I...
...DON'T FEEL SCARED ANY-MORE...
BECAUSE WITHIN YOUR HANDS, YOUR BODY, YOUR HEART...

...THERE'S A PROMISE I CAN BELIEVE IN.
Graduation Ceremony
CONGRATU-LATIONS ON YOUR GRADUATION...
...MU-TSUMI-SEN-PAI.
THANK YOU, EVERY-ONE.
YOU GRADU-ATED IN NO TIME.
STARTING NEXT WEEK, YOU'RE GOING TO KYOTO, HUH?
EAH.

SIGH
しゅん…

KAE-
CHAN.
は
GASP
I…
I'M
FINE!

MU-
TSUMI
SEN-
PAI!!
JUST
KNOW
THAT IF
YOU LEAVE
SERINUMA
ALONE,
I'LL TAKE
HER FOR
MYSELF!
ひし!
FWIP
NANA-
SHIMA-
SENPAI…
GIVE IT A
REST…
Now's
not the
time!
PLIP

THAT'S
FINE,
'CAUSE
IT WON'T
HAPPEN
!!
CONFIDENT
SPARKLE
ピカー
URK
!

IF SERINUMA-
SAN SEEMS LIKE
SHE'S GONNA
FLIP OUT AGAIN,
I'LL SEND HER
YOUR WAY BY
HELICOPTER.
THANKS
!
Just
leave it
to me!
My
eyes!
My
eyes!
I told
you!

TAKE CARE.
YOU, TOO ...
...IGA-RASHI-KUN.
SEN-PAI...
THERE'S SOME-THING I'VE DECIDED TO DO.
ZSH
I...
I'M GONNA GO TO THE SAME SCHOOL AS YOU!!

HUH?
But your grades aren't good by any standard, Serinuma!
ISN'T THAT SCHOOL PRETTY INTENSE ...?!
YEAH !!
WHICH IS WHY I'M GONNA STUDY LIKE MY LIFE DEPENDS ON IT!
THAT'S MY DREAM RIGHT NOW, SO...
I'M GONNA MAKE SURE IT COMES TRUE!!
SO GO ON AHEAD WITHOU ME...
AND JUST WAIT A YEAR...
I'LL JOIN YOU!!
OKAY!
I'LL BE WAITING.

I'LL BE WAITING...

Book: Today's Meal

NO EVENTS NO DOUJINSHI
DON'T GO, OR ELSE YOU'RE DEAD!
日本史用語集
Welcome hooome!

Book: Japanese History Glossary

Book: "A Certain Somewhere" Culinary School

I'M FINALLY HERE!!
I'VE BEEN WAITING FOR YOU.

Seven years later...

OH!!
OVER HERE, NANA-SHIMA-SENPAI!
Waiting Room
for Guests of the Bride and Groom
OH, GOOD. WE MADE IT ON TIME...
SHUFFLE
PANT
SHUFFLE
YOU GUYS ARE CUTTING IT CLOSE!
WHAT TOOK YOU GUYS?
WELL—!!
THIS PUNK FORGOT THE INVITATION AND GIFT MONEY!!
PANT
SO WE HAD TO GO BACK!
IT GOT LOST IN ALL MY LUGGAGE...
THAT'S WHY I'M ALWAYS TELLING YOU TO CLEAN UP YOUR ROOM! I KNEW YOU WERE GONNA PULL SOMETHING LIKE THIS!
YOU REALLY KNEW?!
Ugh! Such a careless kid, honestly

THEN IT'S YOUR FAULT FOR MAKING ME HOLD ON TO IT, NOZO... NANASHIMA-SENPAI!
GRR
HUH? DON'T TURN THIS ON ME!!
IRK
THOSE TWO...
I HEARD THEY'RE ROOMMATES, OKUSAMA.*
SEEMS LIKE IT. I'VE HEARD AS WELL...
MUSE
MUSE
MUSE
MUSE
IT'S ALL THE MORE SUSPICIOUS THAT THEY AVOID TALKING ABOUT DETAILS...
I MEAN, LIKE... NANASHIMA-SENPAI IS A CHEF WHO WANTS TO MAKE IT ON HIS OWN, AND SHINOMIYA-KUN WANTS TO BE A MODEL, RIGHT?
RIGHT, THOUGH?! WHAT KIND OF PERFECT BL SETUP IS THAT?! INCREDIBLE.
RIGHT?
Y'know... NO ONE WOULD'VE THOUGHT THAT SHINOMIYA-KUN WOULD BECOME A MODEL!
AND ONE WHO DRESSES IN WOMEN'S CLOTHES, NO LESS!
Nooo!
RIGHT?!
IT ALL STARTED WHEN HE WAS SCOUTED IN UNIVERSITY, RIGHT? TO THINK THAT PRINCESS USAMIMI IS STILL ALIVE AND WELL!
Such a surprise!
UNLIKE BACK IN THE DAY, HE'S LOST ALL HIS INHIBITIONS!
I SWEAR SOMETHING MUST'VE HAPPENED!!
OH, MY! HO! HO! HO! HO! HO! HO!
HAI HAI HAI HAI HAI HAI
HEH! HEH! HEH! HEH! HEH! HEH!
NISHINA-SAN, YOU SHOULD DRAW SOMETHING BASED ON THOSE TWO!
OH! BY THE WAY!
THEY'RE DOING THE FOURTH SEASON OF "THE STEADFAST GIANT TREE," AREN'T THEY? CONGRATS!!!
EEK!

*In Japanese, *okusama* refers to a married woman.

OH MY GOD, I'M SOOO EXCITED!!
EEK
EEK
I'm totally into the platoon leader!♡
Quite the discerning eye!♡
THANK YOU SO MUCH, AH-CHAN-SENPAI!♡
OH, THERE'S A PREVIEW SCREENING THAT'S COMING UP. WANNA GO TOGETHER?
WHA?! ARE YOU SERIOUS?!
I WANNA GO!! I CAN LEAVE MY DAUGHTER WITH MY HUSBAND, SO IT'LL BE FINE!!
TMP
LET'S GO! LET'S GO!!
NO CAN DO, NISHINA-SENSEI.
THAT'S THE DAY OF THE DEADLINE.
I...I'LL JUST FINISH IT THE DAY BEFORE!!
I can get you in, though.
Whaaat? Boooo!
HAH! IF YOU CAN EVEN DO THAT, SURE!
HAVE YOU EVER FINISHED AHEAD OF SCHEDULE? HMM, SENSEI?!
HAHA
GRRR.
HA! HA!
HA! HA!

IT'S HARD TO BELIEVE THAT IGARASHI-SENPAI IS THE SUPERVISING EDITOR FOR MANGA-ARTIST NISHINA-SENSEI.
Yeah...
I MEAN, IGARASHI WANTED TO GO INTO SALES.
SHRIEK
SHRIEK
Summary
SOMEHOW, IGARASHI GOT ASSIGNED TO THE MANGA EDITING DEPARTMENT, AND HE ENDED UP SUPERVISING NISHINA, WHO WAS STILL WAITING FOR HER BIG BREAK.
OUT OF SHEER DESPERATION, THE TWO ENDED UP CREATING A MEGA-HIT SERIES THAT IS THEIR COMPANY'S MOST WELL-KNOWN WORK TO THIS DAY.
No way!
No way!
I've seen you do this!
Be more aggressive, you silly woman!!
I'm gonna have you groveling before me, just you watch!!
Gimme your worst!
We did it!
units sold
~Reunion~
IT'S LIKE A SKIT!!
GLARE
NO, WE DON'T!!
THEY HAVE QUITE THE CONNECTION, DON'T THEY?
WOW! THEY'RE EVEN IN SYNC!
BA-HAH!
HA! HA! HA!
HEY, YOU GUYS!!
PRIM
THANK YOU ALL FOR TAKING THE TIME TO ATTEND!!
HUH?
WHO'S THAT?!
OH, SERINUMA'S BROTHER...!!
OH, TAKURO-SAN. HELLO!
YOU'RE WORKING FOR THE GOVERNMENT NOW, RIGHT?
SLICK 'N' SHINY
THAT'S RIGHT. STABILITY IS TRULY NUMBER ONE, YOU GUYS!!
HE OVERDID IT WITH THE HAIR!!

SPEAKING OF BROTHERS, WHERE IS MUTSUMI'S BROTHER ...?
Is he not here yet?
KAZUMA? HE'S IN INDIA RIGHT NOW.
HUH ?!

APPAR-ENTLY, HE QUIT HIS JOB ONE DAY, AND NOW HE'S BACK-PACKING AROUND THE WORLD.
YEAH—!!
So fun!
TH... THAT'S WAY TOO FREE-SPIRITED...
I'M JUST RELIEVED THAT GUY DIDN'T END UP BEING A TEACHER !!

MUTSUMI-SENPAI IS WAY MORE SUITED TO BEING A TEACHER. IT'S HIS LIFE'S CALLING, DON'T YOU THINK?
SERINUMA-SAN MAKES ANIME CHARACTER MERCHANDISE, RIGHT?
YEAH! SHE'S PROFITING FROM HER HOBBY!
Ha! Ha! Ha!
NOOO!
AHHH! KAEEE!
WAAAH
OH, QUIET! PULL YOUR-SELF TOGETH-ER!
OH, I'M LOOKING FORWARD TO SEEING SERINUMA-SENPAI IN HER WEDDING DRESS. ♡
Right.
Yeah.
WE GOTTA TAKE A LOT OF PICTURES !!
I BET SHE'S BEAUTI-FUL.
Especially today!
EVERYONE, THANK YOU FOR WAITING.
NOW PRESENT-ING THE BRIDE AND GROOM!
CREAK
...!!

キイイイ…
CREAK
EVERY-ONE!
THANK YOU FOR COMING TODAY!!
?!

S... SERI-NUMA?! WHY ARE YOU... I MEAN... TODAY!! OF ALL DAYS!!
IT'S DÉJÀ VU...!!
BOOM
HUH? WHA?! BUT YOU WEREN'T LIKE THIS WHEN WE MET THREE MONTHS AGO!
HEH HEH! I GUESS I ATE A LITTLE TOO MUCH! ☆
A LITTLE ?!

WELL, MY DOCTOR TOLD ME TO EAT.
HUH? YOUR DOC-TOR ?!
WHAT DO YOU MEAN?! IS SOME-THING WRONG ?!
NO, NO.
FSH
BEAM
HE SAID THAT I HAVE TO EAT...
...FOR TWO NOW!
WHAAAAAAAAA?!

Welcome our Wedding
Nishina-san made this, huh?
So precious!!
Well, this ceremony had a special case, so...
Though the bride ended up looking like a different person altogether...
You made this seating chart, didn't you, Nakano-san?
You're quite talented.
Yeah! It's Mirage Saga themed. ♡ And I go by Yamashita now.
Oh, right.
I'm glad that I have a cute little sister now. ♡ Congratulations! ♡
From Kazuma.
muffy
Muffy-chan telegram...!! They're brothers, all right!

HEY, ASUMA-KUN.
YEAH?
THE HIGH SCHOOL LIFE WE ALL SHARED...
...SEEMS LIKE IT HAPPENED ONLY YESTERDAY...
...AND ALSO QUITE A LONG TIME AGO.
CELEBRATING RIGHT NOW...
...WITH EVERYONE GATHERED HERE...
...AND HAVING YOU BY MY SIDE, ASUMA-KUN...
I'M SO HAPPY.
CONGRATS!
CONGRATULATIONS!

CONGRATS!
YEAH.
I FEEL THE SAME WAY.
CONGRATULATIONS!
THANK YOU.

I'M SO GLAD TO HAVE KNOWN YOU ALL!!

HEY, PAPA.
WHO'S THE BIG WOMAN IN THE PICTURE?
HM?
THAT'S YOUR MAMA.

NO WAY! SHE LOOKS SO DIF-FERENT!!
IT'S REALLY HER.
THIS WAS WHEN SHE TRANS-FORMED SO SHE COULD PROTECT YOU INSIDE HER TUMMY.
Just kidding!
HUH?! NO WAY!!
MAMA CAN TRANS-FORM?! SO COOL!!
Whoa.
HEH HEH.
KUM

YOU MIGHT HAVE A CHANCE TO SEE HER LIKE THAT AGAIN SOMEDAY.
Interview with Bokémon Z Bikachu #19 Actor TAKERU MITSUBOSHI
WOW!!
LOOK.
THIS IS A PHOTO WE TOOK AFTER YOU WERE BORN BECAUSE PEOPLE INSISTED.
OH, AND THAT'S DEFINITELY MAMA!
PAPA! PAPA! HOW 'BOUT THEM? WHO ARE THEY?
THEY'RE MAMA AND PAPA'S FRIENDS.
YOU'VE MET THEM BEFORE, TOO.
A long time ago.
HUHHH? I DON'T REMEMBER!!
'CAUSE YOU WERE YOUNG.
I HOPE YOU GET TO MEET THEM AGAIN.
THEY'RE IMPORTANT PEOPLE.
OHHH.
HEY, YOU TWO!!
I'M READY!! LET'S GO SHOPPING!!
Turn off the TV, okay?
OKAY!!
OKAY!

LET'S GO, SHION!
KAY!
C'MON!
Mirage Saga
THE END

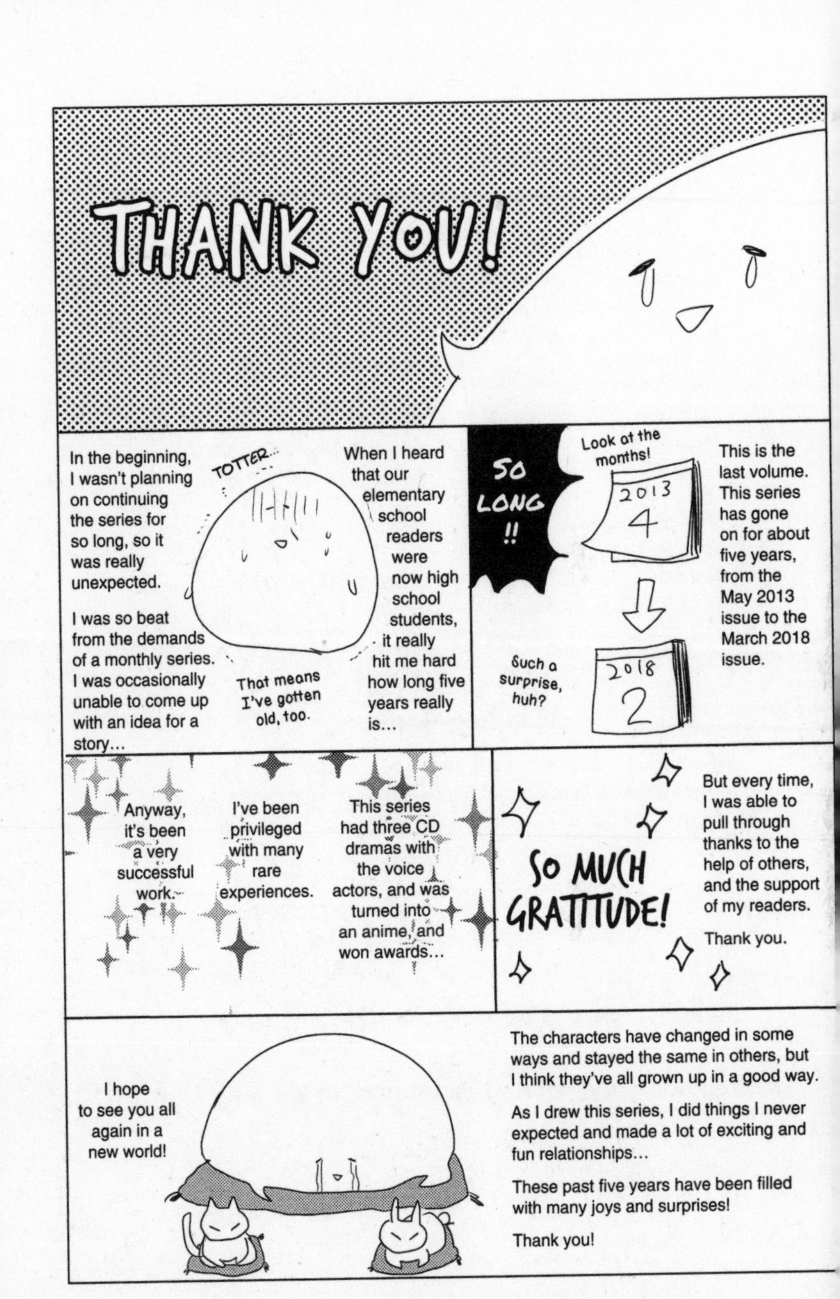
THANK YOU!
In the beginning, I wasn't planning on continuing the series for so long, so it was really unexpected.
I was so beat from the demands of a monthly series. I was occasionally unable to come up with an idea for a story...
TOTTER...
That means I've gotten old, too.
When I heard that our elementary school readers were now high school students, it really hit me hard how long five years really is...
SO LONG!!
Look at the months!
2013 4
2018 2
Such a surprise, huh?
This is the last volume. This series has gone on for about five years, from the May 2013 issue to the March 2018 issue.
Anyway, it's been a very successful work.
I've been privileged with many rare experiences.
This series had three CD dramas with the voice actors, and was turned into an anime, and won awards...
SO MUCH GRATITUDE!
But every time, I was able to pull through thanks to the help of others, and the support of my readers.
Thank you.
I hope to see you all again in a new world!
The characters have changed in some ways and stayed the same in others, but I think they've all grown up in a good way.
As I drew this series, I did things I never expected and made a lot of exciting and fun relationships...
These past five years have been filled with many joys and surprises!
Thank you!

STAFF

Aki-san... You worked so hard on the background and screentones for the longest time!
Shiroe-san... Thank you for the detailed screentone work and delicious food!
Rokku-san... Your backgrounds were always so high in quality!
Yuki-san... Thank you for all the detailed data work you did.
Uzuki-san... Even when all the data was left to you, you did a perfect job!

Shinohara-san... Your backgrounds were always high quality and fast!
N-chan... No one had a better sense for screentone than you.
N-san... From the beginning, you helped me in numerous ways.

SPECIAL ADVISOR
Eiki Eiki-sensei

Thank you for always offering the right advice and story ideas.
I wouldn't have been able to continue if it weren't for you.

Supervising Editor Y-san

I appreciate all your help from the beginning of the series to the very end. Sorry for all the trouble I put you through! And thank you!

Thanks also to everyone else who helped!

And to everyone who stuck around 'til the very end...

THANK YOU SO VERY MUCH!!!

AUTHOR'S NOTE

THE FINAL VOLUME!
THANK YOU SO MUCH
FOR WATCHING OVER
KAE AND THE CREW FOR
ALMOST FIVE YEARS!!!

ALL MY GRATITUDE,
JUNKO

KiSS HiM,
NOT ME!

Translation Notes

Gift money, page 149

Japanese events and ceremonies tend to be highly formalized, and weddings are no exception. Regardless of the style of wedding (Christian or Shinto weddings are both acceptable and common), it's traditional to give gift money (*goshugi*) to the bride and groom if you've been invited to their wedding. The act of giving gift money is structured in a fairly rigid manner, and you are expected to gift anywhere between the equivalent of $300-$1000 depending on your age and relationship to the bride or groom.

Shion, page 164

Due to the use of Chinese characters (*kanji*), Japanese names can sound the same but have different meanings. In this case, "Shion" is made up of two kanji ("history" and "garden"), but that first kanji is not the typical one used for this name (the most common one means "purple"). There is no official reason given for this, but the choice to use a different kanji may have been influenced by Mutsumi's love of history.

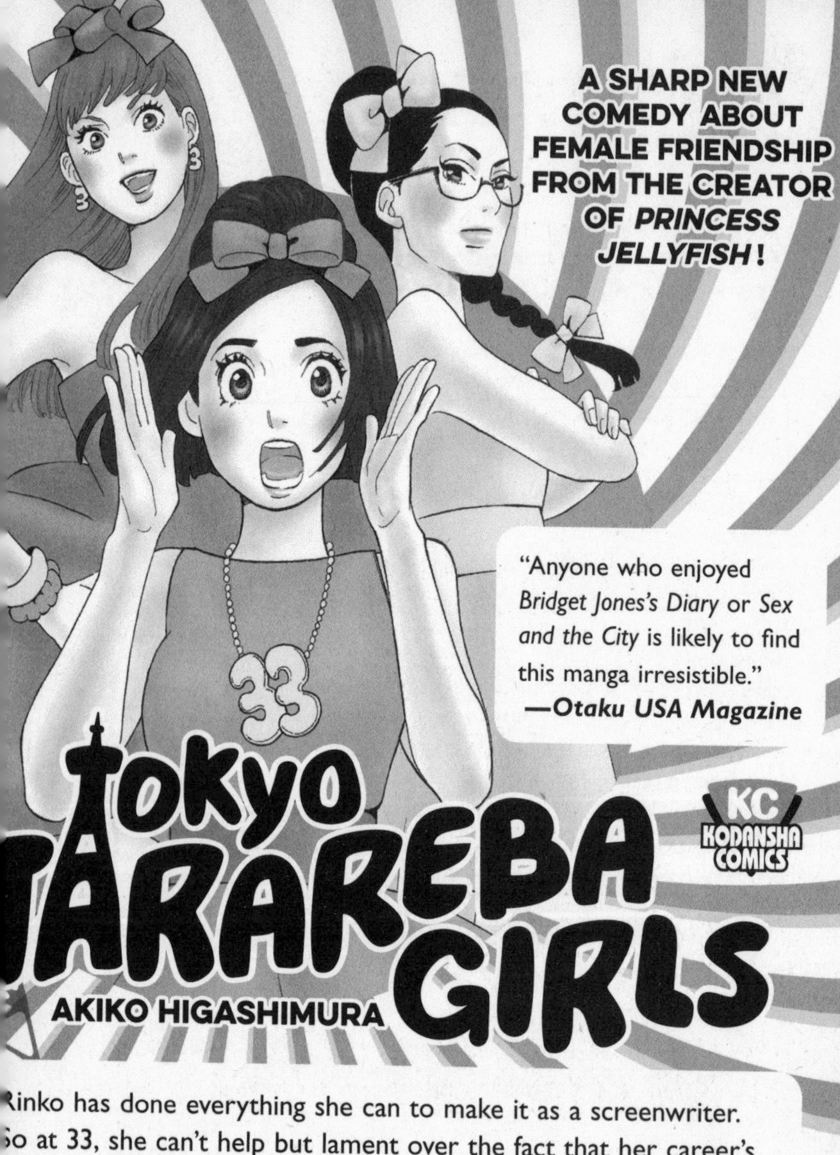

Rinko has done everything she can to make it as a screenwriter. So at 33, she can't help but lament over the fact that her career's plateaued, she's still painfully single, and spends most of her nights drinking with her two best friends. One night, drunk and delusional, Rinko swears to get married by the time the Tokyo Olympics roll around in 2020. But finding a man—or love—may be a cutthroat, dirty job for a romantic at heart!

26-year-old Nagisa Kataura has a secret. Transforming into her favorite anime and manga characters is her passion in life, and she's earned great respect amongst her fellow cospayers. But to the rest of society, her hobby is a silly fantasy. As demands from both her office job and cosplaying begin to increase, she may one day have to make a tough choice—what's more important to her, cosplay or being "normal"?

Narumi has had it rough: Every boyfriend she's had dumped her once they found out she was an otaku, so she's gone to great lengths to hide it. At her new job, she bumps into Hirotaka, her childhood friend and fellow otaku. When Hirotaka almost gets her secret outed at work, she comes up with a plan to keep him quiet. But he comes up with a counter-proposal: Why doesn't she just date him instead?

WAITING FOR SPRING

A sweet romantic story of a soft-spoken high school freshman and her quest to make friends. For fans of earnest, fun, and dramatic shojo like *Kimi ni Todoke* and *Say I Love You*.

KISS ME AT THE STROKE OF MIDNIGHT

An all-new Cinderella comedy perfect for fans of *My Little Monster* and *Say I Love You*!

LOVE AND LIES

Love is forbidden. When you turn 16, the government will assign you your marriage partner. This dystopian manga about teen love and defiance is a sexy, funny, and dramatic new hit! Anime now streaming on Anime Strike!

Kiss Him, Not Me volume 14 is a work of fiction. Names, characters, places, and incidents are the products of the author's imagination or are used fictitiously. Any resemblance to actual events, locales, or persons, living or dead, is entirely coincidental.

A Kodansha Comics Trade Paperback Original.

Published in the United States by Kodansha Comics,
an imprint of Kodansha USA Publishing, LLC, New York.

Publication rights for this English edition arranged through Kodansha Ltd., Tokyo.

First published in Japan in 2018 by Kodansha Ltd., Tokyo, as *Watashi Ga Motete Dousunda* volume 14.

ISBN 978-1-63236-557-6

Printed in the United States of America.

www.kodanshacomics.com

9 8 7 6 5 4 3 2 1

Translation: David Rhie
Lettering: Jacqueline Wee
Editing: Haruko Hashimoto
Kodansha Comics edition cover design: Phil Balsman